out of sight, out of mind?

homeless women speak out

Anwen Jones,
Centre for Housing Policy,
University of York

CRISIS

WORKING
FOR
HOMELESS
PEOPLE

Crisis is the national charity for single homeless people – those who have no legal right to accommodation. Our objective is to ensure no-one has to sleep rough. We take practical action to help all single homeless people move towards a secure, sustainable home.

We provide aid at all stages of homelessness, from outreach workers helping long-term rough sleepers to access the services they need, to deposit guarantee schemes enabling homeless people to find homes in the private rented sector.

Crisis works with local groups across the UK, building on their grass roots knowledge, local enthusiasm and sense of community.

The research and interviews for **Out of Sight, Out of Mind?** have been undertaken for **Crisis** by the **Centre for Housing Policy, University of York**.

Published by **Crisis**, 1999.

Crisis
Challenger House
42 Adler Street
London E1 1EE

Registered Charity no. 1036533
Telephone   0171 655 8300
Facsimile   0171 247 1525
E-mail   crisis.uk@easynet.co.uk
Internet   www.crisis.org.uk

ISBN 1 899257 38 1

For a full list or to order any publications, please contact
Crisis on 0171 655 8300 or visit the Crisis website, www.crisis.org.uk

Printed and bound by Biddles Ltd. Typesetting by wave. Cover printed on Parilux

CONTENTS

FOREWORD by Shaks Ghosh   v

Introduction   1

PART ONE **Becoming homeless**

1. Early lives and reasons for homelessness   **5**
Early lives   5
Reasons for homelessness   6
Women with children   11

PART TWO **Being homeless**

**2. Seeking help, staying with friends and relatives
     and sleeping rough**   **15**
Being homeless   15
Seeking help   17
Sofa surfing – staying with friends and relatives   22
Sleeping rough   24

3. Living in a hostel   **35**
Life in a hostel – views and opinions   35
Getting by   45

PART THREE **The future**

4. Moving out and moving on   **51**
Waiting to move out   51
Preparation for moving on   54

Acknowledgements   57
The author   57
The photographs in this book   57

Foreword

> It's horrible sleeping rough, scary, especially when you are young... you feel really vulnerable, you don't sleep because it is so shitty and dangerous. It's like you've lost your hard shell and you've only got a soft inner shell so people can get at you easier.
>
> *Kate, aged 28, Bristol*

When I first read our research *Out of Sight, Out of Mind – The experiences of homeless women* – I found it depressing reading. Explanations of why people end up on the streets, including reference to domestic violence, family breakdowns, mental health problems and more. All of this set against figures which show that the number of women on the streets is increasing. But what also struck me was the tremendous spirit of homeless women and their determination to move on.

This is why we decided to draw on the stories of our interviewees. In their own words, through direct quotes, in this supplement to the main research women describe what is like to be on the streets and live in hostels. It forms part of our Homeless Voices series. For too long, homeless women's voices have been overshadowed by the majority of people on the streets – men. Today women's prospects in the general population have never looked better. So why is this hidden minority so obviously losing out?

In *Out of Sight, Out of Mind – Homeless women speak out* we look at some of the stories behind conclusions of the main research. Their voices are powerful and can help inform the work of the government, policy makers, those who provide services and members of the general public who may wonder why anyone has sleep rough in the first place. In particular, we hope this book will provide a stark illustration of what it is like for women to sleep rough.

Shaks Ghosh

Shaks Ghosh,
Chief Executive, Crisis

> You're trying to keep normal, looking on the bright side you know.
>
> *Jackie, aged 19, Liverpool*

Introduction

This supplementary report presents the findings of a study of women's homelessness in the words of homeless women themselves. Seventy-seven interviews were held with women who were or had been homeless in hostels and day centres in London, Bristol, Liverpool and Brighton during the summer of 1998. These areas were chosen for several reasons, including the number of women who were or had been sleeping rough in the area and the number of homelessness projects that have contact with women.

Background to the study

Recent research has suggested that the number of homeless women is increasing and that more young women are using hostels, night shelters and are sleeping rough. Although there has been a great deal of interest in homelessness in recent years, very little is known about the experiences of women.

The study

In April 1998, Crisis commissioned the Centre for Housing Policy at the University of York to conduct a study of women's homelessness.

The aim was to explore how women became homeless and what it was like to be a woman sleeping rough or living in a hostel. It asked how women coped, whom they turned to for help, what services, if any, they used and their experience of provision for homeless people.

Full details of this study can be found in the main report *Out of Sight, Out of Mind? - Women's experience of homelessness.*

PART ONE
Becoming homeless

CHAPTER 1

Early lives and reasons for homelessness

This chapter looks at the early lives of women and their lives before they became homeless. Many of the women had led disrupted lives, some had been placed in local authority care, some had suffered abuse from their families. A few women felt that they had never really had a home. Other women had led settled lives until some crisis occurred and they became homeless. Many of the women interviewed had been homeless before, some from an early age and a number of them had more than one experience of sleeping rough as youngsters.

Early lives

I started running away [from care] when I was nine...I used to run away for a night and then they'd take me back.

Sally, aged 23, Liverpool.

I wasn't happy at home. I was abused by my stepfather...he used to beat my mother. She didn't believe that I was being abused. I used to run away from when I was 14. I'd stay out for a few nights but then the police would take me home but then I'd do it again.

Lynne, aged 53, London.

Reasons for homelessness

Women were asked what was the main reason for their present or most recent episode of homelessness. The most common reason given was domestic violence; among younger women it was being thrown out by their parents. Women gave a number of other reasons for their homelessness, including eviction or loss of tenancy, breakdown of relationships, discharge from hospital and prison, abuse from family, illness and return from abroad.

Domestic violence

This reason was given most often by women in their thirties. However, other women said that they had been homeless in the past because of the violent behaviour of a partner. Some of the women said that their partner's behaviour had suddenly worsened but in some cases women had endured violent relationships for years before finally deciding to leave. One woman said she had left her husband a number of times and had slept rough in the past but had returned home. This was partly because she had a son but also because she had no money.

> Because I am a woman I had no income...I walked a long way and then got a taxi to London, I paid him with a cheque that I knew would bounce. I slept on the pavement for four nights...and I would have slept rough until I found somewhere to go even if it had taken longer. I wasn't going back, not this time.
>
> *Kathleen, aged 50, London.*

Thrown out by family

> My mother just threw me out...she accused me of taking drugs and stealing. She just threw me out. I had to go and stay with friends and then the council put me in bed and breakfast.
>
> *Emma, aged 16, Brighton.*

> My mother threw me out because of arguments, basically we couldn't get on...My mother gave me two weeks to find somewhere, then I had to go. I had to doss on friends' floors, doorsteps if they were out, for two and a half weeks.
>
> *Hayley, aged 19, Brighton.*

> My mother threw me out, she's an alcoholic and she used to pick on me. Things got worse when my sister left home.
>
> *Charlie, aged 17, Brighton.*

It was not only young women who were made to leave their homes, one woman had been living with her sister.

> My nephew was on drugs and his behaviour was getting worse. In the end he threatened us and threw me and my daughter out.
>
> *Moira, aged 54, London*

Eviction and loss of tenancy

In many cases, women said that the reason for their homelessness was eviction or loss of tenancy, but their stories were often complicated.

I came here first because of my ex. I lived with him for six months and he was OK at first but then he started to get nasty. I got thrown out of my flat because of him, he broke in and smashed the place up after we finished. I got my things and went to a friend's, then I found a bedsit and he did it again. He used to follow me around, hitting me, spitting on me. I slept in my car then so he couldn't find me. I did that for three or four months.

Stephanie, aged 26, London.

I was evicted because of noise and rent arrears and then the washing machine leaked into the flat below, well that happened more than once. And my boyfriend caused trouble.

Ruth, aged 26, London.

I stayed with the council for about ten years. Then they stopped my benefits so no-one paid my rent but I didn't know because I was away...I lost all my belongings everything except the clothes that I was standing in.

Sarah, aged 29, Bristol.

Illness and discharge from hospital

I was ill and I had to leave my home...The Social Security said they'd pay my rent and help with the mortgage if I made a contribution. Six months later I found out it hadn't been paid and I received a repossession order. The mortgagors don't want to wait for back payments.

Annie, aged 41, London.

I was in detox for six months, then I went into a B&B but got thrown out 'for not being sick enough'. I slept rough my husband [estranged] was away, he would have helped me but friends didn't want to know.

Marjorie, aged 50, London.

Leaving prison

I'm homeless because of drugs, shoplifting, in and out of prison. I've been to several places before this and been thrown out of them all, for being violent basically. I've only ever had one place of my own, a one-bedroomed flat with three kids. So it's a vicious circle really.

Sharon, aged 40, Liverpool.

I spent a year on remand in Holloway and then Styal and then Mornington Crescent [probation hostel], then I went back on the drink, slashing my wrists so I was homeless again.

Lynne, aged 53, London.

Breakdown of relationships

Most of the women who gave this as a reason for their homelessness were young women who chose to leave home because they had 'had enough'. It is often suggested that young people leave home 'for the bright lights' without considering the consequences. The research found that most young women were well aware of the problems they might face, yet felt they had little choice but to leave.

> I left home because I wasn't getting on with my mother. I've got three younger sisters and I was expected to look after them. Being the oldest in a one parent family I didn't have a life...I love my mother to bits but I think things would have got a lot worse if I'd stayed at home. My mother leaned on me too much, she used to tell me everything...I used to feel guilty about going out with friends, I'd come home early to make sure everything was OK. My schoolwork was suffering too. I did feel really guilty about leaving home. I felt terrible and thought about going back but I had to make myself do it so I could have a life.
>
> *Sophie, aged 18, London.*

> I left home when I was 17 or 18. I couldn't stand living at home. I felt like a lodger. It was a two-bedroomed house and I had a brother and a sister. My sister slept with my mother so I had to share with my brother [who was 15]. I wasn't going to do that so I slept on the couch. I didn't get on with my mother either...I was on a YT scheme one time, well I should have been but my mother wouldn't lend me the fare. It was a brilliant placement on a farm but I didn't have the money to get there I didn't get benefits because of my age and when I did get some money my mother wanted £20 out of my £35...I just went to the shop one day and thought 'fuck it' and didn't go back.
>
> *Mel, aged 21, Liverpool.*

Abandoned tenancy

> When my brother died I didn't handle it too well. I split up with the children's father and started going out, getting drunk and falling asleep anywhere. All I needed was a bit of help but someone reported me to social services and said I was on drugs. I was smoking hash but I wasn't on heroin or crack. They were going to take my children into care, they are now but with my parents. None of this did me any good, living without the children with all their things around in the flat. I got into hard drugs. I just walked out and started staying with friends because the flat depressed me. I lost my flat and ended up on the streets, I abandoned my flat.
>
> *Caron, aged 32, Bristol.*

Women with children

Although the research focussed on single homeless women, many of them, like some of those quoted above, had children who had been placed in care. Some women had to leave their children behind when they left a violent partner, others said that they had been unable to cope and placed their children in the care of social services or with relatives. Other women left their children with relatives while they slept rough or stayed with friends because there was not enough room for them all. One woman said she had slept rough with her children and they had been taken into care.

> My son went to foster parents while I hit the road...I went to the battered women's place in Chester...My social worker didn't want me to take him. I've met other women in refuges, in hostels or dossing and they have kids in care. They've all been told that once they have a home the kids can come back, but it isn't that easy.
>
> *Mona, aged 54, Liverpool.*

PART TWO

Being homeless

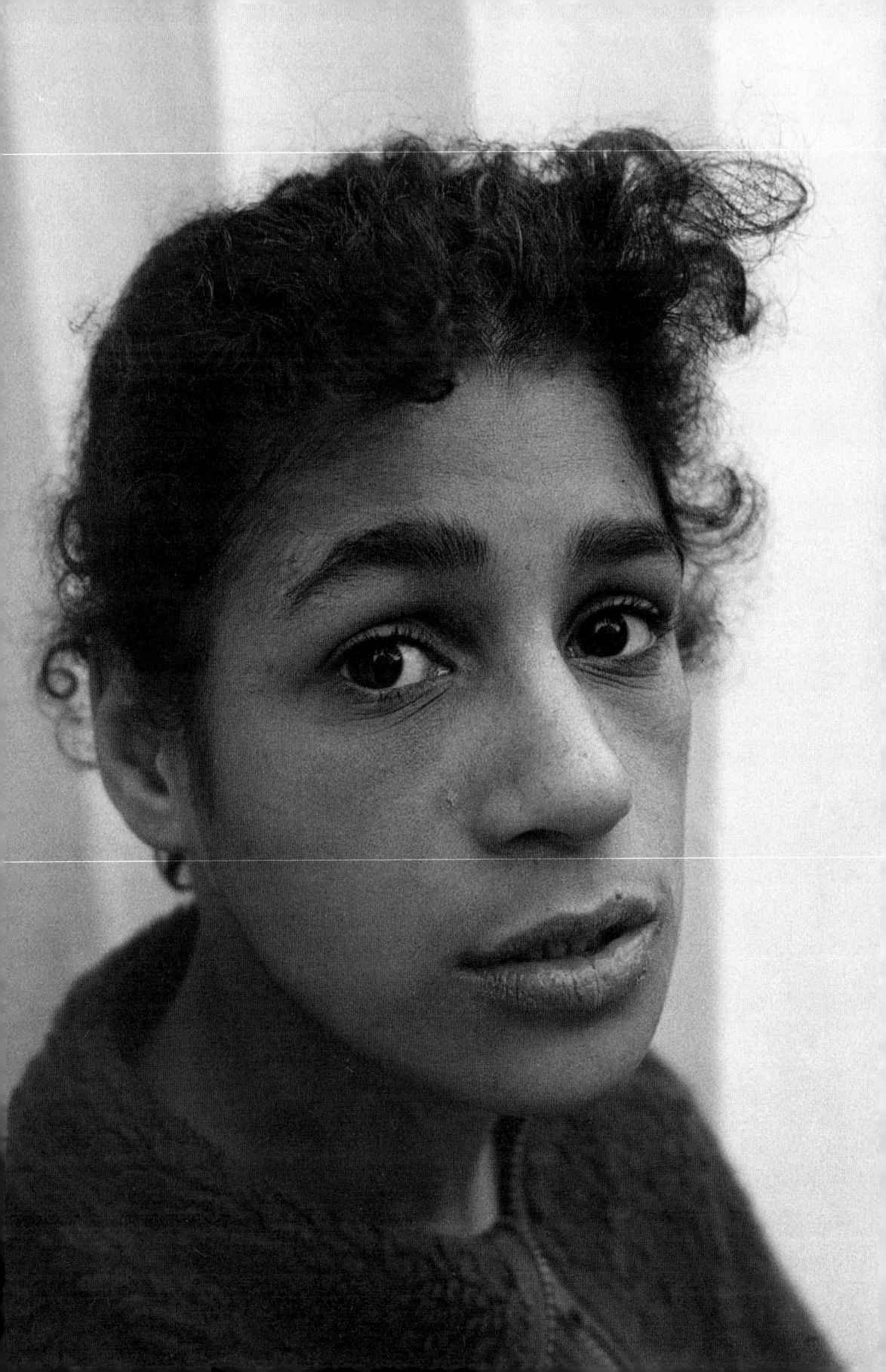

Seeking help, staying with friends and relatives and sleeping rough

This chapter begins by describing how the women felt when they became homeless and what women did when they first became homeless, where they went for help and the sort of help, if any, they received. It then goes on to describe the experience of staying with friends and relatives and of sleeping rough. The final section considers the impact of homelessness on women's health.

Being homeless

How does it feel to be homeless?

> A few years ago I did a course and that looked at homelessness, I knew nothing about it. I thought homeless people were tramps. Of course it isn't like that at all, it's shocking, frightening. You feel vulnerable, it really hits you, what are you going to do, you feel lost.
>
> *Ally, aged 41, London.*

> When my mother threw me out...I didn't want to tell anyone but I was scared that I'd have to sleep rough and I had all these nervous rashes.
>
> *Charlie, aged 17, Brighton.*

Losing possessions

Women also described the experience of losing all, or nearly all, of their possessions when they became homeless. Some women who had left violent partners were too scared to return for their belongings, others had friends or relatives who collected some of their possessions for them. Some of the women who had been evicted had placed their belongings in storage but this was expensive and women were worried that if they did not keep up the payments their belongings would be auctioned. Usually women who had to leave in a hurry lost almost everything. Women who had been homeless before or had slept rough for some time tended to say that possessions were not very important, as one woman said 'you get used to leaving things behind'. Other women found it very distressing.

> My landlord changed the locks and I didn't know what to do, I lost everything I ever owned. All my belongings, photos, I even lost my address book. I don't even remember what I had now , well I try not to think about it because it is too painful. It's like losing half your life, like you never existed. I had lovely things, coats I bought in Harrods' sale and look at me now, everything I own is second hand.
>
> *Georgina, aged 40, London.*

> I didn't believe I would be evicted, I didn't pack anything. I left with the clothes I stood in.
>
> *Maria, age unknown, London.*

> I didn't see all my belongings out on the street but my neighbours told me.
>
> *Ruth, aged 26, London.*

Seeking help

People usually become homeless with little or no warning, with no time to arrange alternative accommodation, to ask for help or advice or even to pack belongings. At the time when they became homeless most women had little knowledge of the help available although most knew of some advice agency. Women approached a variety of agencies and organisations for help. These included housing departments, the Department of Social Security, Social Services, housing advice centres, homelessness charities, Citizen Advice Bureaux and housing associations. They also approached less obvious sources including the Samaritans, railway station staff, student counsellors, ministers of the church and the police. One woman explained that she went to the police because it was an emergency. Some women had no idea where to go for help or found themselves homeless at weekends or bank holidays when offices were closed.

> I slept for two nights on Euston station. I asked if I could sit on Victoria Station, somewhere I wouldn't get mugged, but I was refused. No-one told me where to try, not one person told me about hostels or tried to help really. A policeman suggested I try Euston as it's a bit more upmarket. I thought I'd ask the station manager. I waited to see the manager and then a cleaner came along and told me to go. I had the bright idea of getting arrested, I was a shivering, starving wreck, in tears by now. I was told I couldn't stay where I was by security but in the end they let me stay for two nights...This has been a real education because I could never understand people sleeping on the streets, I thought they were crackers, stupid people. There's the Salvation Army and millions of hostels but you can't get into them, they're all full. It's really difficult.
>
> *Kay, aged 40, London.*

> I slept in a launderette, locked in safely. It was a bank holiday weekend, Easter I think, a long one. Then I stayed in public toilets, that was disgusting, draughty and smelly. I had some money on me but I had to be careful.
>
> *Marjorie, aged 50, London.*

Even when there was some help available women did not know about it and there were practical difficulties to overcome. These women became homeless in London.

> You're in a trap, in a cycle, but one day you have got to have help but there is nowhere to go, no-one to tell you that there is help.
>
> *Chris, aged 37, London.*

> I was sleeping on the stairs in a block of flats...My brother suggested hostels, someone suggested the Salvation Army and I started thinking dormitories, cockroaches, damp and of war time. As it was summer I thought I'd hang on. I went to Westminster Council who gave me a list of hostels, I didn't even have the money to 'phone them. I had no idea that you could go to a hostel and get your rent paid.
>
> *Mercedes, aged 34, London.*

> We wandered around for two nights, slept on the [railway] station in January. We had no belongings. I didn't have my medication...It was freezing and it didn't do my health any good. We went to the police station because it was an emergency and they gave us a number for a hostel helpline. But we didn't have any money to get there. We had to get a crisis loan to come down to the hostel.
>
> *Moira, aged 54, London.*

The women who had the widest knowledge of provision were those that had been homeless the longest, especially those who had slept rough and had used day centres, hostels, night shelters and soup runs in the past. They learned what was available from other people who were sleeping rough. There were women who had slept rough who had little or no contact with agencies until recently and few women said they had contact with outreach teams. Some women did not want any contact with official agencies as they were scared of being sent home or back to care. Others had asked for help in the past but found agencies unhelpful and decided to manage alone, even if this meant sleeping rough. As one woman said 'I wouldn't go to the Social in the end as they cause more trouble'. A few women said that they did not look for help immediately because they were past caring. Eventually, though, these women had all sought help.

> I think you get scared as you get older because you have more sense. It started getting more worrying, if you go to sleep are you going to even wake up or wake up with a gang of men trying to rape you. So it was getting concerning and my health.
>
> *Victoria, aged 32, London.*

I just accepted being homeless, it's just something that happens but I got sick of sleeping rough and I went to the YMCA. I knew someone who lived there...I got fed up when the gang broke up and I was on my own. I'm not sure what happened to them, one was a smackhead and died, another was on gas and went to a high dependency unit, one went to Leeds and I don't know about the others.

Mel, aged 21, Liverpool.

Young women (aged under twenty) were fairly well informed. Some said that they had learned about homelessness in school and some had friends who had been homeless. Their knowledge probably prevented many young women from having to sleep rough.

I did PSE at school. We covered bullying, relationships, violence and homelessness. We had guest speakers including people who had slept rough and a homelessness worker so I knew where to go. I was used to going to the council with my mother...I went to the council and told them I was homeless. I'd been to a 'down and out' centre, a day centre in Baron's Court to look at the London Hostels Directory. The council told me to go home, I said I couldn't and they referred me back to the project at Baron's Court. I asked to look at the Hostel Directory there and found the hostel.

Sophie, aged 18, London.

Other women complained that agencies did not seem to care when they went for help or advice. Young women were often told to return home and women who were staying with friends, usually in over-crowded conditions, felt that they were not being taken seriously. Many women felt that officials look down on homeless people.

I felt worse because I had made myself homeless. The attitude was 'you've made your bed you sleep on it'. The fact that you haven't got a bed is immaterial. It wasn't just me that felt like that, I was told that I had made myself deliberately homeless.

Kay, aged 40, London.

I found one DSS man very abusive, he thought he could swear and be abusive because I was homeless and used to it. I try not to take any notice but people do look down on you.

Ally, aged 41, London.

Other women had found agencies sympathetic. Even though they could not offer suitable accommodation they provided some practical help.

I had no money, no food for three days. I went to DSS and this man took pity on me and gave me £10 for food. They did find a children's home for me but I couldn't go there, not after living on my own.

Louise, aged 17, Brighton.

Sofa surfing – staying with friends and relatives

Most women who had friends or family in the area had stayed with them for a time when they first became homeless and many women spent a long time living with friends or relatives, moving from one to another, often with periods of sleeping rough in between. All the women who stayed with friends or relatives said that this could not be a long-term arrangement, that although friends and relatives were usually willing to help this could cause problems for them.

When my mother threw me out I just thought what am I going to do? I went and found my friends and stayed with one. It was really nice at first but I couldn't stay forever. I hated sleeping on floors, not being able to have a shower when I wanted. I lived with a friend for a couple of weeks and then couldn't stay there any longer so moved from friend to friend kipping on their floors. Then I moved in with my boyfriend but then he got sent down. I lived with his friend but I was overstaying my welcome. Then I slept rough, in parks and on the beach. I didn't really have anywhere to go.

Louise, aged 17, Brighton.

You can only stay with friends for so long if you want to keep them. My friend turfed her son out of his bed for me. You can't live like that, it wasn't fair on them.

Kay, aged 40, London.

I wouldn't have been able to stay with my friends for long as they were getting hassle from their neighbours who said they would tell the council, or my other friends had children and there was just no room.

Ruth, aged 26, London.

Some women said that when they had become homeless friends changed towards them, or tried to take advantage of the situation.

> I had to leave my house because I was ill, I'm a manic depressive and I was very ill, I think I might have killed myself. I went to stay with friends... I slept on the couch for five and a half months, I had to wait for them to go to bed. I was told I could stay for five months and then things started going wrong, my friend wanted my freezer, then my TV, things from my house...I couldn't get to sleep one night because the daughter came in late and watched a video. It was all too much so I left.
>
> *Annie, aged 41, London.*

> When I first became homeless a pupil's father and my boss were 'kind' to me, offered me somewhere to stay, I was raped by one and the other tried to rape me. They thought they never had a chance before because I was decent, I had a job and I had a flat well [they thought] she's not so decent now is she, she's got no-one and nowhere, she has to be grateful.
>
> *Georgina, aged 40, London.*

Sleeping rough

Sleeping rough was described as a horrible experience and one which no-one would want to go through again. Women slept on railway stations, in park shelters and in public toilets; in cars, on staircases, in back gardens, and on doorsteps; in barns and on buses and beaches. Everyone agreed that sleeping rough was extremely unpleasant. Some women said that they had learned a lot from the experience. For others sleeping rough was the first step in making a new life for themselves. These were women who had left abusive or unhappy relationships or had run away from care.

> It's horrible sleeping rough, scary, especially when you are young. You feel OK at first, free, but you're not because it is so shitty. You feel really vulnerable, you don't sleep because it's too cold and too dangerous. It's like you've lost your hard shell and you've only got a soft inner shell so people can get at you easier.
>
> *Kate, aged 28, Bristol.*

> I ended up on the Strand. I turned into an alcoholic. I used to live on the Strand or the Bullring. Everyone sort of looked out for everyone else, there was a real sense of community. It felt, well it was a bit shitty really, I was only a kid [14]. I had no trouble sleeping because I was drinking.
>
> *Trish, aged 27, London.*

> In some ways being homeless has made me stronger. I've been mugged and insulted and taken advantage of but some people have been kind.
>
> *Victoria, aged 32, London.*

It was horrible sleeping rough, it was freezing and you couldn't wait for the morning for the day centre to open, that was a help. I used to sleep near these air shafts, all nice warm air, behind buildings, hospitals. You used to get moved on by the police...I didn't have the money for a bed and breakfast and there weren't any hostel places.

Lynne, aged 53, London.

In a sense some of these women were lucky, at least there was somewhere warm to go for food. In many smaller towns and in rural areas there was no help available at all.

I slept rough for about 18 months. It was a very bad winter. I used to carry plastic, newspapers like a proper bag lady. I'd sleep in barns, hedges, anywhere to get warm but I would also be drunk. One night I got nice and settled in a snowy hedge, I had a drink and went to sleep as warm as toast then the police woke me up and put me in the cells. What for, drunk in charge of a snow drift? The police never offered me any help...I'm not the healthiest of people, mostly through drink though but it had more of an effect on my mental health. I felt absolute despair. Who can I go to for help, who can I talk to, who'd want to talk to me looking like this? In the end you don't care. There aren't a lot of people sleeping rough around there and there's no provision. I didn't know of anywhere or where to ask.

Mona, aged 54, Liverpool.

There was nowhere for homeless people there. If you are homeless in small towns then you really are homeless.

Kathleen, aged 50, London.

> I left home November and slept around until January. I went home at Christmas but then went back to sleeping in friends. I did go to Social Services but they didn't have anywhere for me. Then I had nowhere to go at all, I used to sleep in the park shelter with my boyfriend's mate. I had to come to Brighton, it was the only place Social Services could find me.
>
> *Louise, aged 17, Brighton.*

Keeping safe

Although the women who had slept rough said that they had been very scared, few of those who had slept rough for only a short period (one night to a week) said that they had bad experiences. This was probably due to the precautions they took such as staying close to other people or simply not going to sleep. Women, especially when they were alone, chose to sleep somewhere hidden away or to walk around all night as it was safer. It is quite likely that head counts of people sleeping rough on the streets miss many women.

> I slept rough for a few days at a time. I might end up at a friend's house for a couple of weeks. I didn't stay out for long in London. You can't walk around and feel safe, you just can't go to sleep, you have a choice, sleep with one eye open, walk around or do drugs. You're scared of the time it takes to wake up properly – it could mean the end. Also there are people on drugs and booze who don't care and will rob you.
>
> *Patsy, aged 19, Brighton.*

> I just walked around all night near my house. I felt safer nearer people I knew.
>
> *Alison, aged 30, Liverpool.*

> I was raped twice. The first time I was woken up by a gang of men and attacked.
>
> *Trish, aged 27, London.*

Women who slept rough for longer periods somehow managed to adapt to their situation. In some cases they made friends with other people sleeping rough or learned about day centres where they could go for a wash and a change of clothes. However, few women said they used these facilities, instead they managed as well as they could on their own. Women who had friends or relatives nearby often left their clothes in their homes and went there during the day for food and to wash and change. Most women went to great lengths to take care of their appearance.

> I used to go for a shower to the leisure centre but I got told off because the showers were meant for people using the facilities, so I went and bought a swimming costume and paid £2 to go for a swim so I could be clean.
>
> *Maria, age unknown, London.*

> There were public toilets nearby which we called our own private bathroom, it was nice and clean. We used to go there for a stand up wash, we never looked as if we were sleeping rough. We made sure that we had two changes of clothes. There was a launderette nearby and the woman there let us do our washing for nothing...We were too proud to walk around looking rough.
>
> *Beth, aged 18, Brighton.*

I used to sleep rough on and off when I was working [in the 1960s]. Sometimes I'd sleep with clients, stay the night or sleep in an entry or back garden. I didn't have any belongings, I used to go to the public baths and then buy second hand clothes from the rag and bone man. It saved carrying clothes around, they'd get all creased. I didn't want to look scruffy even though I was homeless. There is no need for it, there are showers and that.

Lynne, aged 53, London.

Other people's attitudes

The attitude of other people on the street varied. Some women reported verbal abuse, being hit or being spat on, and having food and drink thrown at them, but many told us about acts of kindness from complete strangers. Most women said that people look down on those who were homeless; that people assumed they must have done something wrong. A few women said that this is what they thought until they became homeless themselves.

You do get treated badly. Just because you're down they think they have the right to spit on you or throw a can at you. It's probably worse being a woman because men assume you are easy or take advantage which is really degrading. Many times I've felt like a piece of meat.

Victoria, aged 32, London.

Some people were nasty, I had a couple of slaps from people I asked for money. Most people were sound. Most people were OK. They'd give you money and that. Some idiots would be nasty 'get a fucking job' like…I had company when I was sleeping rough, I met up with an old fellow who had slept rough for years and he lent me his sleeping bag.

Mel, aged 21, Liverpool.

This man gave me £16, he saw me crying on the pavement and he gave me money after I said I haven't got any money, I haven't got anywhere to live…Then I met this woman and she let me stay and gave me some numbers for hostels.

Kathleen, aged 50, London.

Night shelters

Night shelters were seen as a last resort when it was very cold or wet and there was nowhere else to stay. Night shelters were described as relaxed because there are fewer rules and regulations than in many hostels but this meant that night shelters were also chaotic and often dangerous places. Night shelters often housed the most unstable homeless people and people who 'were so down or so drunk or on drugs that they are past caring'. Only one woman had anything positive to say about night shelters apart from the fact that they provided somewhere warm and dry and a bed.

I like not being told what to do…I'd prefer to be in a night shelter except that they steal your things.

Sonia, aged 27, Bristol.

Other women who had stayed in night shelters thought that they were dirty, rough, lacked privacy and security and said they would never want to stay in one again. Some women said they would never consider staying in a night shelter but these were mainly women who had not slept rough for long periods or had not slept rough during the winter.

I'd heard so much about them from people I've met and from television programmes I wouldn't go to one. I preferred to sleep rough.

Marjorie, aged 50, London.

There was a shelter but there wasn't any room, I didn't fancy it anyway as it had a bad reputation. I slept out for a week in May but it was still cold at night. Thank God it wasn't raining.

Louise, aged 17, Brighton.

Hostels, I went but they only had emergency accommodation for three nights...I went to [night shelter] it was awful, rats, dirty...awful. People were fighting and stealing. I stayed one night and left, I'd rather sleep outside. They stole what little I had including my bus pass.

Maria, age unknown, London.

Health

Few women complained of illness caused by their homelessness but few of them had spent very long sleeping rough. Those women who had slept rough for months at a time complained of a number of conditions such as respiratory problems, aches and pains and chilblains which they associated with sleeping rough. Many women said that they started drinking more alcohol or using more drugs when they became homeless or were threatened with homelessness.

> It was being homeless that made me drink and led to my health problems...I had no trouble sleeping because I was drinking...Then I got rather ill – through alcohol, liver fucked, kidneys fucked, ulcers, really bad. I had pancreatitis. I've also got a bad chest and I've got chilblains. I did begin to think what am I doing here, and that is when I started doing the hostel system.
>
> *Trish, aged 27, London.*

In terms of their mental health, most women felt that although becoming homeless had been a distressing and extremely worrying experience, hostel life was more stressful. A number of women said that they had suffered depression, mood swings and insomnia and were being prescribed anti-depressants, others said that they were drinking more alcohol or taking more drugs.

> It's difficult in the hostel but I am smoking more crack now and doing less heroin so that's quite good. My health is getting worse, my doctor's told me I won't see thirty unless I change my lifestyle.
>
> *Donna, aged 22, Bristol.*

Access to health services

Many women slept rough or stayed with friends close to their former home and were still registered with their own GP. Other women who had moved away from their home area and were not registered with a doctor did not see this as a problem as routine health checks were the least of their worries. Few women said they had problems accessing health services but many women who slept rough did not worry about their health or try to access services until they had to.

> The only doctor available was at [drop in] and it was disgusting, infested, blood and needles on the floor. Some day centres had all sorts coming in, alternative therapists. There's not much health care for the homeless. I had to go to UCH when I was ill, that was the usual homeless hospital for people on the Strand. They can be funny, like 'Why don't you go to see your own GP?' 'Because I don't have one.' 'Why don't you have one?' 'Because I haven't got a home.' But they did see you eventually. They left me waiting for ages. I still didn't have a GP, I was treated but in Outpatients.
>
> *Trish, aged 27, London.*

CHAPTER 3

Living in a hostel

This chapter presents women's experiences of living in hostels, what they liked and disliked about hostel life. We then consider the impact of homelessness on women's health, their employment and their income.

Life in a hostel – views and opinions

The women had different views and opinions about living in hostels but there were also some common complaints. For women who had been sleeping rough on the streets and women who had spent months, even years, sleeping on friend's floors or on sofas, hostels were a 'lifeline'. Women were grateful for things that most people take for granted.

> I've been sleeping around friends' places a long time now, a long time...Now I think of this place as home. I've got my own room for my own things, there's a place to buy food and there's baths and showers so you can be clean and change your clothes. There's loads of advantages. And there's a bed, there's always your bed to go to. When you've slept on a sofa for years and years can you imagine what a bed feels like?
>
> *Sarah, aged 29, Bristol.*

At the end of the day it's a roof over your head. I see these people sleeping rough and I thank my lucky stars. If they hadn't had room for me...well I try not to think about having nowhere to go.

Rita, aged 62, London.

I wanted to kiss the woman who accepted me, it was too good to be true. I was crying, I was so grateful. I thought it was like an hotel, there was a fridge, bed, basin and all new furniture.

Mercedes, aged 34, London.

I like it here, it has saved me. I expected the hostel to be a lot rougher. I was very surprised and pleased. They were all very friendly and we are all in the same situation, some are from abroad and have to start all over again. When you are being hit you just want to get away. You do miss things at first but knowing all these people helps. They are homeless like me and they are genuinely nice people.

Kathleen, aged 50, London.

As the earlier comments suggest, women were extremely relieved to find a hostel place, especially when their only alternative was sleeping rough. However, hostel life was not always a pleasant experience and it was one which was making women ill. The type of hostels for homeless women vary. Some are small homely units housing only half a dozen women, others are large hostels housing over 100 men and women. Large institutions could be quite daunting, especially for younger women.

You can't choose your friends when you are homeless, there are people here, you don't know who they are and generally you wouldn't have anything to do with them if you weren't homeless. You have to be careful, don't get too involved. In a hostel people begin to lose their social skills, some don't care, some get angry and others get so depressed they top themselves.

Ally, aged 41, London.

Although women tried to consider others living in the hostel and often said they worried about them, it was not always easy to be tolerant, especially when there appeared to be no hope of moving out for some time. In most hostels women referred to other residents, who worked, as prostitutes. This was generally accepted as part of hostel life. One woman living in a direct access hostel described the hostel as a 'cross between a psychiatric ward, an old people's home, a rehab and a brothel'. This caused many problems for the women; they were propositioned by men outside the hostel and on the telephone. Women said that these men assumed that if you were homeless and living in a hostel then you must be a prostitute.

You're trying to keep normal, looking on the bright side you know. Then a girl comes in desperate for a fix but she couldn't be bothered to fetch her condoms. I went to her room and got them for her to save her going out without protection. She'd get £10 – enough for a fix.

Jackie, aged 19, Liverpool.

> The prostitutes come in after being raped but they go back out the next night. A lot of them say they don't want to but need the money. They don't all spend it on drugs. Some girls go out and work and come back with a KFC, fags and sweets.
>
> *Sam, aged 21, Liverpool.*

Two women said that the behaviour of residents almost made them return home; one of these women had left a violent husband. A few women had thought about sleeping rough again.

> It's an experience. Given the choice of living in a hostel or living on the streets I still haven't decided which is worse. I have actually thought about sleeping rough again but I'd have to start all over again. I am making an effort.
>
> *Victoria, aged 32, London.*

A common feeling among the women interviewed was that they had enough problems of their own without having to cope with other people's problems.

> When I first moved in I couldn't believe the place, what went on. Then I started to mix after a while. I asked this woman for a ciggie and she started telling me all her problems, about her mental health, being on the game and it scared me. I didn't ask her for a ciggie again.
>
> *Jackie, aged 19, Liverpool.*

Some of the women said that they had 'got used' to hostel life and had started to think of it as normal. Women said they were picking up what they thought of as bad habits such as asking for money or cigarettes, something they would not have done before becoming homeless. A group of women in a large mixed direct access hostel said that almost everybody took drugs and most female residents were prostitutes. One of these women admitted that this was very worrying as she was beginning to think that this was 'what life was supposed to be like'.

> People's attitude when you say you live in a hostel. It's a very nice hostel but I prefer not to say I live in a hostel. It puts people off but anyone can end up living in a hostel.
>
> *Jane, aged 37, London.*

> I think a lot of people that moan about people living in hostels tar us all with the same brush, they don't for a minute think that we never thought we'd end up homeless. They think we must have all gone down the slippery slope and that it's all our own damn fault.
>
> *Sharon, aged 29, London.*

> I think people withdraw when they find out that I live in a hostel, they think I must have done something bad, I'm getting older so I must be a prostitute...I have become isolated, even in church people think badly of me. Because they've got homes and a family they don't seem to understand.
>
> *Georgina, aged 40, London.*

Drugs and alcohol

One of the problems that many women complained about was the use of alcohol and drugs in hostels. This was a problem for women who were trying to get off drugs and for women who had to cope with people's behaviour. Women complained that some residents spoiled things for others and understood why there were certain rules and regulations. In some hostels, however, rules were broken.

What you get told and what goes on are two different things. We are told that drugs are a no-no but loads of people are on drugs and the staff ignore it. It might be better to have hostels for drug users as people come in here and end up with a habit, I've tried things in here that I never touched before.

Sharon, aged 29, London.

There wasn't supposed to be drugs or alcohol on the premises but there were.

Sophie, aged 18, London.

I am a junkie and I always will be. We're told that drugs are a no-no but there are people on drugs, it's hidden away and the staff ignore it. I came in here [from sleeping rough] to get off drugs and to see it all around makes it very, very hard.

Pam, aged 37, London.

Spending time

A common complaint among women living in hostels was that they had nothing to do and, having little money, they could not afford to spend on leisure activities. Some hostels had day centres attached or provided some form of activity such as computer classes, aerobics, gardening and art classes. One hostel provided a free leisure pass. In most hostels, however, there was little to do except play cards, watch television or play pool. Young women said they stayed up late watching videos or talking, and remained in bed all morning. Some women had hobbies and interests that kept them occupied and a few women did voluntary work. Women who lived in their home area said they visited friends or family. In fine weather women killed time by going for walks or sitting in the park.

The day centre is a great help, you don't feel like socialising when you are homeless so this is good, lots to do to get you doing things, it's heaven sent. Anyone can come in and use the day centre so you get a mix. It's great.

Ally, aged 41, London.

I like to be doing something. The day centre is OK, there are lots of activities but although there are a lot of people coming in there are also a lot of people from the hostel there and you see enough of them anyway.

Victoria, aged 32, London.

Most women appreciated activities provided in the day centre or hostel and others who had nothing to do thought that this was a good idea but again, the longer women spent living in hostels, the more discontented they became.

It makes you feel like nothing that they have got to fob you off with little picnics and that instead of dealing with the real issues. You know if they put the same amount of effort into resettling us and getting on with letting us move on instead of bloody well giving us stupid singing lessons and computers and all that no-one uses.

Mercedes, aged 34, London.

One of the problems in many hostels was that everything was done for residents. Many women said they missed doing 'normal' things such as making their own breakfast and doing housework. Many women would have liked to take on more responsibility and to be more independent but they realised that not everyone would co-operate.

It would be nice to do your own breakfast, but some people wouldn't behave. I'd love to do a Sunday dinner for everyone…I even miss cleaning…People should have the responsibility of cleaning their own rooms, but not everyone is the same, some people can't look after themselves.

Alison, aged 30, Liverpool.

Women living in smaller hostels, especially young women, were responsible for cooking meals, cleaning and shopping for food and this was seen as good preparation for when they moved out to live independently.

Everyone has a job, there's a rota and everyone has to cook one night a week. People don't always do their jobs but house meetings usually sort them out.

focus group, Brighton.

Level of support

Although most women said that hostel staff were doing their best under very difficult circumstances, many felt that they were not receiving the level of support they needed. Others felt that the hostel was not suitable for them or for other residents or that staff 'didn't care'. Women who were drug users and women with mental health problems complained that they were not getting any better.

I reckon by the end of the year I'll be dead. When you have a mental health problem people don't care, they'll give you pills and say you'll feel better in four weeks but you can't wait four weeks...This isn't the right place for me. I need somewhere where they are more into helping me. Here they are too tolerant and just put up with my behaviour. I can sit upstairs drinking and smoking all weekend and no-one says anything. I just feel that if they cared they'd stop me.

Jan, aged 30, Bristol.

It would improve things if someone simply took an interest in my health. I need more support but no-one has tried to find me somewhere more suitable. I don't think this is the right place. I can be left for days to cope alone...I was going mad at home now I do it in the garden here...I'd think it was odd if someone spent every evening walking up and down the garden, but as long as you're not causing any problems or breaking the rules that is OK. I am described as the model resident. Thinking about my dog keeps me under control, if I flipped I'd be sectioned and would lose the dog. I have to keep rolling along, head down because beggars can't be choosers. They've got this real thing about me being 'articulate', like if you are articulate you are OK. 'She's coping'...but I'm not, I'm not fucking well. I never break the rules or argue...I am under so much pressure as well as the pressure of behaving all the time...I feel so frightened it takes my breath away. But because I behave everyone thinks I am fine.

Annie, aged 41, London.

This hostel has excellent facilities, it's much better than most places but when you are in a crisis there often isn't anyone to help. Sometimes you can feel really desperate but unless you are lucky there isn't any support. If you talk to the same person all the time because they are the most sympathetic and helpful you worry that they will burn out.

Sharon, aged 29, London.

I was attacked, mugged, and the staff were brilliant. I think the staff are really caring, if they're not then they're jolly good actors.

Kay, aged 40, London.

Getting by

Employment, benefits and other sources of income

The main source of income for nearly all the women interviewed was Income Support or Job Seekers Allowance and sickness or disability benefits. Very few women had paid employment but a number did voluntary work. Some women said that cash in hand work had been a useful means of supplementing their income from benefits and young women had found casual work in bars and restaurants, handing out fliers, touting for nightclubs or selling newspapers. A few women who had done cash in hand work in the past said that hostel staff were 'cracking down' on people doing casual work because of benefit regulations. One woman who had been homeless many times thought it was easier to get by in the past, although a few women said that they had managed to hold down a job or to attend school or college even when sleeping rough or staying with friends.

> I think it was much nicer and easier to sleep rough in the 1960s...In those days you could find plenty of casual work to get by, in cafes, washing up and the like.
>
> *Lynne, aged 53, London.*

> I managed to work, my boss knew I was sleeping rough so he paid me daily. Sometimes I used the money for a B&B, a bed for the night...but I'd have to go without food.
>
> *Kate, aged 28, Bristol.*

Nearly all the women had work experience and many had vocational qualifications. These included City and Guilds and Btecs, qualifications in nursing and dental nursing and National Vocational Qualifications in hairdressing, beauty therapy, catering, business administration and caring. A few women had been educated to degree level or equivalent. Most of these women thought they would be able to find work when they moved out of the hostel. The reason most women living in hostels gave for not working was that they simply could not afford to because of the high rents charged in hostels. The only woman with a fairly well paid job (working as a practice nurse) said that she was worse off when she worked because she lost her benefits, had to pay her rent and also had to pay travel costs. This benefit trap frustrated women; many said they wanted to work and to be independent. Given the chance to work, they believed they could do something about finding somewhere to live.

> It's £148 a week to stay here, why can't they just give that to us and let us pay for somewhere of our own... When I move out they'll only give me £42.50 because I'm under 25.
>
> *Rebecca, aged 23, Brighton.*

> I've been unemployed, well signing on, for seven or eight months now. I could manage financially doing bits and bobs but...it's maddening, they'll pay £96 for the hostel but they won't pay £55 for a bedsit... If I wasn't signing on there's no way I could afford to stay here...I want to earn enough to be able to pay rent and get somewhere decent.
>
> *Patsy, aged 19, Brighton.*

Some women thought they were not allowed to work while they were living in a hostel and a few said that they actually been discouraged from taking work.

I'm on Income Support but I'm looking for a job, that's how I want to get established again but I've been advised not to work until I've got my own flat because of Housing Benefit.

Kathleen, aged 50, London.

Women also said that work would give them something to do. Day centres and classes were appreciated but women would have liked to spend their days more productively. Another point made by many women was that hostel life was not designed for people with work, paid or voluntary. A number of women said that hostel life was too tiring and too stressful for them to work. One young woman who had a job said that she could not collect her post or do her laundry as facilities were available only during office hours. Other women complained that if they worked late they missed meals and went hungry (the evening meal was often served at 5 or 6 pm).

Most women had to make a contribution towards their rent and found it difficult to manage on the benefits they received and a number of women were under threat of eviction because they owed rent. Other women had not received any money and complained about the length of time taken to sort out their benefits.

The DSS has to be told that the people they need to stop treating like dirt are the most vulnerable, it's bureaucratic madness. I think it should be illegal for them to turn you down for benefits that you are entitled to. The reason they do it, and they do it across the board, is that most people won't take it to appeal. I'm not saying that homeless people and people in crisis should get special treatment but this is ridiculous. I owe £2,000 rent and have been given 28 days' notice. No Income Support, no Housing Benefit.

Sharon, aged 29, London.

Other sources of income

A number of women said that they had begged in the past, especially as youngsters, but few said that they still asked people for money. Some women appeared reluctant to explain how they managed for money when they were sleeping rough although a few said that they stole food and goods when they were younger. The women who had begged said that they had to but it was not something they were very proud of or liked having to do.

> I used to beg, I actually feel rather ashamed about it and I've got a criminal record for begging. I was fined £10 the first time, I had to beg to get the money to pay the fine.
>
> *Trish, aged 27, London.*

> If you have to be out there begging, well people say 'go and get a job', it isn't that easy. When you have to ask for money people look down on you.
>
> *Victoria, aged 32, London.*

A few women said they worked as prostitutes and others had done so in the past. These women, who were working at the time of the interview, lived in the same hostel.

> I get my social every week and every now and again I go out just to help make ends meet.
>
> *Sarah, aged 29, Bristol.*

PART THREE
The future

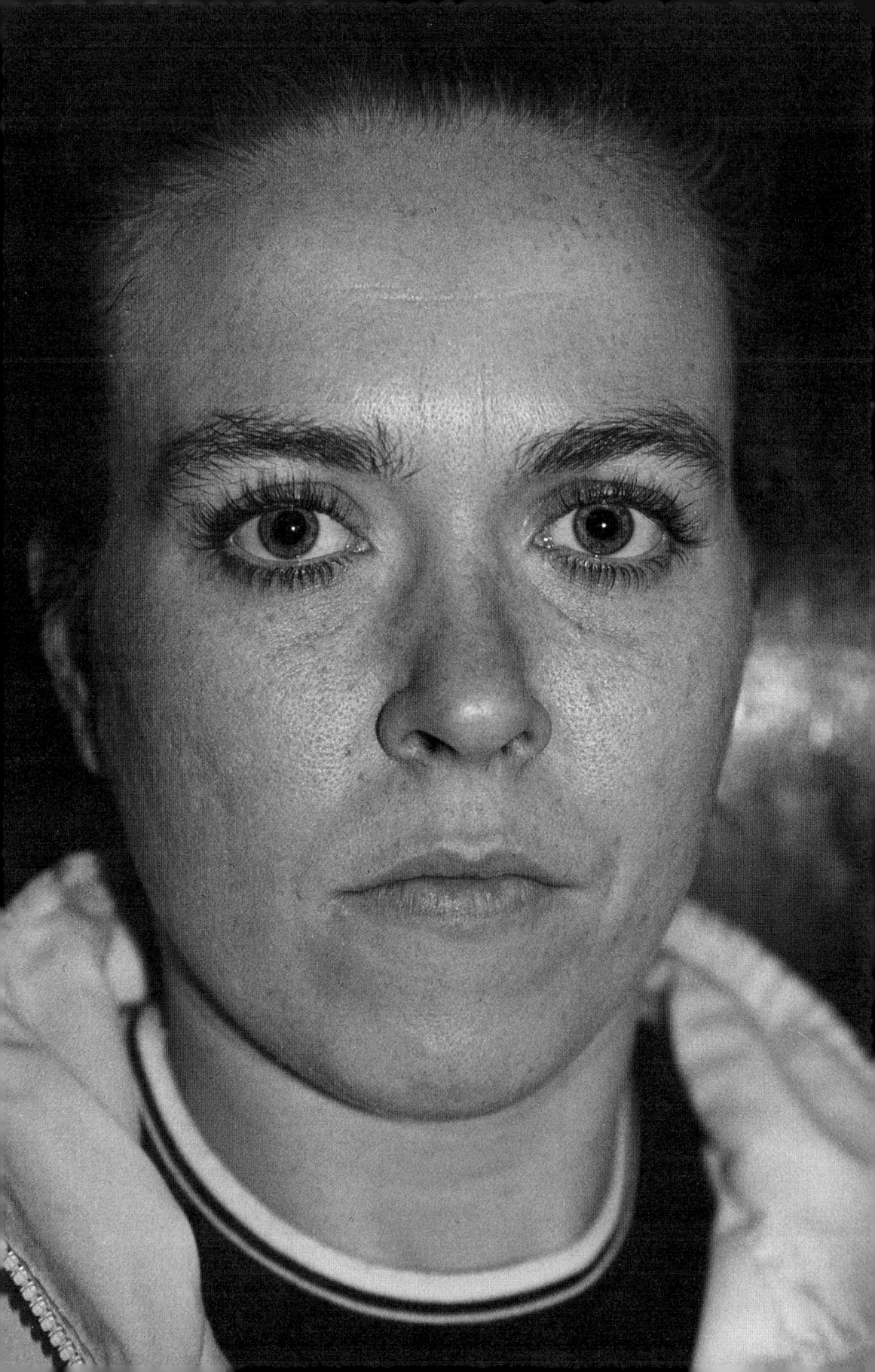

CHAPTER 4
Moving out and moving on

Waiting to move out

> It's like waiting for something to happen that's never going to happen.
>
> *Moira, aged 54, London.*

Most hostels are supposed to provide temporary accommodation until permanent accommodation can be found yet many women had lived in hostels for years rather than months. Many women became very frustrated and depressed because of the long wait for accommodation. They also felt powerless to change their situation and often had no idea what was happening to their application for accommodation.

> I've been here too long now, it's getting me down now. It's getting to the point now that I don't see any end to all this. I've lived here a year and I lived in Holloway for a year and a half, and five months in Barnsbury. Everyone says that they'll find somewhere soon but it never happens.
>
> *Iris, aged 39, London.*

> I've been told to say I slept rough if I'm asked so I'll get a place.
>
> *Karen, aged 17, London.*

I used to go around taking the addresses of all the boarded up houses and the council still said there was nowhere for us.

Di, aged 38, Liverpool.

Selling council houses was a huge mistake, what about single people...This is a very expensive way to accommodate people.

focus group, London.

Almost all the woman interviewed said they wanted a place of their own and only one woman said she would never be able to live on her own and hoped to stay in the hostel. Having a home of their own was seen as the next step in making a new life for themselves and the importance of a home to women cannot be overstated. Women believed that once they had their own flat or house then they could begin to rebuild their lives, to return to work or to education, to begin relationships and in some cases to re-establish contact with their families. Most women felt that once they had a home of their own they would be able to sort out their lives and take control.

My boyfriend kicked me out so often and I had to sleep rough a few times. After a row he'd say 'it's my house, get out'. So that's why I'd like a place of my own – so that I could tell him.

Abbie, aged 20, Liverpool.

Many women said they just wanted to get back to normal, to doing everyday things like cooking, cleaning and even paying bills.

> Back to normal, I'd like to make some money, get a bigger place so that the kids can come to stay. Make a useful contribution.
>
> *Ally, aged 41, London.*

Most women said that they would like to work once they had a home of their own. Those that worked before moving into a hostel were quite confident that they would find suitable employment and few women felt that they would need further training or help in finding work. There were a few women who said they needed help with basic skills, that is numeracy and literacy. There were also a few who said that they had not thought about getting a job and some of those who were claiming sickness or disability benefits did not think they would work again. Many of the women planned to return to their former employment or to similar work and a few planned to enter further or higher education.

The young women were the most optimistic and enthusiastic about their futures but older women were also looking forward to their new lives.

> I worked for a vending machine operator, I was a hygiene operator, but I'm also a trained dental nurse. Once I've got somewhere to live then I'll be motivated to go out and work...I've never felt so useless in my life.
>
> *Mercedes, aged 34, London.*

I would like to get back to the way things used to be, having my own place and being independent. Hopefully I'll get a shared tenancy with my boyfriend. Eventually I'd like to get a mortgage for a nice little place, a maisonette with a garden. I wouldn't like to go back to a high rise.

Ruth, aged 26, London.

I want my own flat and to do a degree in art...Ideally I'd like a one-bedroomed flat with a patio but I don't really mind.

Kathleen, aged 50, London.

Preparation for moving on

Although most of the women interviewed said they would be able to cope on their own and were looking forward to living independently, they would require some help with the practicalities of setting up home such as buying and moving furniture.

They wouldn't give me a loan so I'm scrounging and the hostel is helping me find second hand stuff from charity shops and they'll help me move my things for nothing

Moira, aged 54, London.

It will be just like when I moved out when I was 19, I had to start from scratch, building things up and getting things together, but it was fun then.

Dorothy, aged 47, London.

We are getting furniture and things together now ready for the flat. We've found shelves, a sofa, cupboards, all sorts that were either donated or 'found'.

Trish, aged 27, London.

Although nearly every woman interviewed wanted a home of her own, some admitted to being nervous about the prospect of living alone and it was clear that a number of women would need ongoing support. Sometimes this was because of problems with alcohol or drugs but also because women had become used to hostel life. Some women were worried that they would miss the company and support they had in the hostel and a few women were concerned that they would fall back into 'bad habits' or simply be unable to settle.

I feel much stronger now than I did when I was living on my own. It's nice having people to look after you, no money or bill worries. They give you food vouchers if you are broke...Quite a few people don't want to move, some have been here for years.

Ruth, aged 26, London.

I don't know but I think I'm scared of settling down. I don't think I would stay. I know that moving around isn't sensible but I have to. I begin to feel trapped but then again moving around brings a different set of problems.

Kate, aged 28, Bristol.

Women who had been resettled in their own homes described some of the difficulties they faced adapting to living alone, sometimes for the first time in years.

> It's not easy [living independently] after living in a hostel. You need to pay bills, but I did go to college to learn about housekeeping and so on to see if I could cope. In hostels everything is looked after for you.
>
> *Lynne, aged 53, London.*

> I shared my first flat but most of the time people were moving on or getting thrown out so I was on my own. I got my notice to quit, I hated it there but thought they'd have to find me somewhere to live. But they told me to sort myself out...I was in rent arrears. I tried, I wrote to housing associations but no joy, not enough points. When I only had a few weeks left my psychiatrist helped me and I was offered a bedsit. Now I've got a flat, a semi-independent flat. I've lived there since January [seven months] and I'm getting on all right, I suppose. There have been a few teething problems – with the bailiffs – but nothing I can't sort out but I do get help from here [day centre].
>
> *Mel, aged 21, Liverpool.*

Acknowledgements

I would like to thank Crisis, who funded this research. I am grateful to both Nicholas Pleace and Deborah Quilgars at the Centre for Housing Policy for their expert supervision of the project. I am also grateful to Kate Tomlinson and Julie Alexander of Crisis and Leila Baker of Shelter for their helpful comments and suggestions. This study would not have been possible without the co-operation of the staff and volunteers of the various hostels, day centres and night shelters who agreed to provide a venue for the interviews. Finally I am most grateful to the women who agreed to take part in the group discussions and the interviews. The responsibility for the content of this report lies with the author.

Anwen Jones, Centre for Housing Policy, University of York.

The author

Anwen Jones is a Research Fellow in the Centre for Housing Policy at the University of York.

The photographs in this book

All the photographs in this book have been taken by award-winning photographer Moyra Peralta. We are indebted to her and to all the homeless people who agreed to participate in the photography for this book. To protect subjects' identities, photographs do not match quotes.

out of sight, out of mind?

the experiences of homeless women

Vulnerable women of all ages are stuck in temporary hostels with no hope of a permanent home. Some have to resort to sleeping rough. Over the last two decades an increasing proportion of homeless people are women. So what is going wrong? Despite research on the experience of homelessness, little work has been done to discover how to solve the problem of women's homelessness.

Why do women become homeless? How do they cope? What can be done to enable them to build a brighter future? An analysis of current empirical data is followed by a description of 77 in-depth interviews with homeless and ex-homeless women in London, Bristol, Brighton and Liverpool. The study was conducted by the University of York on behalf of Crisis.

Out of Sight, Out of Mind – The experiences of homeless women is essential reading for policy makers, housing and homelessness professionals, journalists, students, teachers and lecturers in housing and social policy – anyone interested in learning more about the particular needs of homeless women.

ISBN: 1 899257 32 2

£7.50

Words from the street
The views of homeless people today

'Well presented and insightful…a useful source for anyone interested in homelessness in Britian today'

Professor Anne Power, Department of Social Policy and Administration, London School of Economics and Political Science.

This book is the first in the **Homeless Voices** series, which provides a platform for the views of those sleeping rough in Britain. It features open interviews with homeless people: how they arrived on the streets, how they cope, their views on solutions to homelessness and their aspirations and hopes.

For policy makers and housing professionals, as well as all those with an interest in homelessness, **Words from the Street** gives a candid portrait of life for Britain's homeless people. It provides valuable advice on how to shape policy to ensure it meets their real needs.

The research was conducted for Crisis by the London Research Centre.

ISBN: 1 899257 18 7   Price £7.50

To order, contact:
Crisis, Challenger House, 42 Adler Street, London E1 1EE
Telephone 0171 655 8337
Fax: 0171 247 1525
e-mail: crisis.uk@easynet.co.uk
Internet: www.crisis.org.uk
Please add £2 post and packing per order.

Homelessness Factfile 1998/99

'I warmly welcome this book, which brings together data in a handy form, to help us focus on the main issues that face us'
Hilary Armstrong MP, Minister for Housing and Local Government.

A new digest of accessible statistics, research and information about single homelessness – updated every two years. **Homelessness Factfile** will include a stand-alone discussion on an area of current interest. This edition covers the impact of changes in housing benefit on homelessness.

Part of the **Homeless Facts** series, this book is for policy makers and housing professionals in the statutory and voluntary sectors, as well as journalists, academics and students. **Homelessness Factfile** will, for the first time, provide up-to-date information on homelessness in a single volume.

The research was conducted for Crisis by the London Research Centre.

ISBN: 1 899257 19 5   Price £6.50

	Quantity	Price	Total
Words from the Street	402	£7.50	
Homelessness Factfile 1998/99	403	£6.50	
Plus postage and packing* (£2.00)			
Cost of order			

I would also like to make a donation to Crisis of: £

Total enclosed £

Please copy this page and send with your name, address and payment details to the address overleaf. Orders will be despatched within 14 days.

Feedback questionnaire

Please fill in the sections that are relevant to you (on both sides) and return to Crisis, Challenger House, 42 Adler Street, London El IEE.
Fax: 0171 247 2993

This form may be cutout or photocopied.

Have you discovered anything new or do you have any new thoughts/opinions about homelessness and/or homeless people from reading the book? If yes, what?

The person whose comments I found most appealing was:

because:

Are there any issues covered in the book that you would like to read more about?

☐ I would like to order a copy of *Out of Sight, Out of Mind? – The experiences of homeless women* (£7.50 + £2.00 p&p)

☐ I would like to order another copy of this book (£4.50 + £2.00 p&p)

☐ Please invoice my organisation

☐ Cheque payable to 'Crisis' enclosed

☐ I would like to know more about the **Homeless Voices** series

☐ I am interested in receiving information about other aspects of Crisis' work

☐ I would like more information on how I can support Crisis

Name	
Organisation	Position
Address	
Tel	Fax
E-mail	

Please send details of this book to my colleague:

Name	
Organisation	Position
Address	
Tel	Fax

Thank you for taking the time to feedback your thoughts and comments.

Faxback: 0171 247 2993   Email: sasha.chisholm@crisis.org.uk